Crone's Wines

Crone's Wines

Late Poems

BY

Margaret Rockwell Finch

WORD GALAXY PRESS
An imprint of Able Muse Press

Acknowledgments

"Ringwood Valley" was previously published in *The Lyric*.
Many thanks to Nancy Randolph and Marta Rijn Finch for their
generous help in preparing this manuscript for publication.

Also by Margaret Rockwell Finch:
Davy's Lake
The Barefoot Goose
Sonnets from Seventy-Five Years

Writing a foreword to what is evidently Maggie Finch's last book of poems is a bittersweet experience. My mother's poems have been the most enduring of the three central pursuits in her life (the other two being visual art, particularly fine art doll-making, and genealogy). Her poems have also been an enduring thread in my own life since the day I announced to her at thirteen—she loves to tell the story—that I wanted "to be a *real* poet, like Millay or someone." Maggie believes that I used the phrase "real poet" that first day to distinguish my hoped-for path as a published, publicly known poet from her own more private one. But of course, Maggie's poetry, though her previous three volumes have all been self-published within our family, is entirely real.

Starting that day in 1969, Maggie and I exchanged drafts of our own poems and critiques of each other's poems fairly consistently for about twenty years, until I became a mother myself, and more sporadically after that. And just as she was there for my poetry as I grew, offering praise and critique and believing in my work, I was there for her beautiful, haunting poetry as well, eventually helping bring it to print in books, anthologies, and a textbook, and to discussion at a critical seminar on women's poetry at the West Chester Poetry Conference.

As Maggie (she asked her children to call her that in her high-feminist period in the late 1970s, when she went back to college) writes in her preface, she came from a literary family and began to write poetry early. She often recounted the story told in the interview below about dictating her first poem to her mother. The resounding rhythm of the little black manual typewriter she'd had since she was a teenager, ricocheting through the house as she swung the return bar back at the end of each line, was a familiar sound when I got home from school as a child. From my youngest days I remember seeing her writing notebooks filled with extravagant yet tidy flourishes arranged in lines with some words carefully crossed out, often in blue or red marker, and lists of rhyme words squeezed into the margins. I remember how she would work at a poem, typing draft after draft until it was just right, and then using smudgy black carbon paper to make final copies to send out to editors. I remember how she sang her poems sometimes to little tunes that had come into her head as she was writing them. I remember going to meetings of the Poetry Society of America with her in New York City during the 1970s, witnessing her frustration at the increasing hegemony of free verse—and her ultimate triumph, with family and friends in attendance at the Awards Dinner, when they awarded a prize to her beautiful early lyric, "So In the Mind":

This is the lake
Where the deer come bending
Heads fearful and slow—and break
Surface of sky and branches
Blending:
So in the mind
By word slowly spoken
By mouth fearful and kind
Is the surface
Broken.

Though Maggie loved to share her new poems and often had specific questions to ask such as my opinion of a choice between two words or ending-lines, I remember her as a stubborn poet. She often refused my carefully considered editorial suggestions—though, I admit, I sometimes found her refusal to accept my suggestions frustrating—modeling for me an inspiring attitude of creative self-sufficiency and self-trust. Another poetic lesson I recall from her is the advice, delivered during a critique of my first villanelle when I was eighteen, that "if you're going to do a form, you may as well do it right." This was excellent advice on structure, which she herself followed on the level of the poem and also on the level of the book. I recall, for example, how much care and pleasure she took in assembling the seven sections of her first book of poems, the 182-page collection *Davy's Lake,* which I published for her in 1996.

Maggie had a caressing, reverent way of sharing her favorite poems and passages of poetry aloud, as if she were petting one of her many cats. The poems I remember her reciting with most relish were Yeats's "The Lake Isle of Innisfree," Hopkins's "Binsey Poplars," and favorite lines of Millay:

> Love in the open hand, no thing but that,
> Ungemmed, unhidden, wishing not to hurt,
> As one should bring you cowslips in a hat
> Swung from the hand, or apples in her skirt,
> I bring you, calling out as children do:
> "Look what I have!—and these are all for you."

Herbert, Crane, Bogan, and Glück were other favorites, and she especially treasured the mysterious openness of Edwin Muir and W.S. Merwin. Early in her marriage, under pressure from my father, she had "tried to write like T.S. Eliot," as she put it, and had produced magnificent poems on "serious" (she'd pronounce the word with a degree of mockery) topics such as the settlement of the United States and Hiroshima. But by the time I came along, her poetic voice had moved defiantly back into more personal territory.

Crone's Wines was a title Maggie had been planning for many years to use for what she said would be her last book (another title she considered was *Heard at the Hinges*). Many of these poems were composed in her eighties, when she was widowed and living alone in a historic home on the Kennebec River, 1463 Washington Street in Bath, Maine. Maggie had always loved nothing more than to linger in bed writing poems and reading. Now, freed of her five children (the "five lovely ships" of "In My Mirror") and two husbands, with her eyesight too poor to make any more dolls, she focused on her poetry and nothing else for perhaps the first time since adolescence. That yellow house she loved so deeply, with its views of the river and visits from her neighbor, William Hayes Brown, a retired English teacher and the final love of Maggie's life, provides the setting and the inspiration for many of these poems.

Like the poems in Maggie's beautiful earlier books, the poems in *Crone's Wines* often inhabit liminal spaces: hinges, corners, edges, and sunsets; silences, secrets, and moments of unspoken, dawning wonder; and the mysterious reflective moments in which pieces of furniture, or houses, or memories come half alive, while living people take on the archetypal dignity of the dead. In style, the poems inhabit liminal spaces as well, balancing between free verse and form, meditation and song. Maggie's lyric voice in this volume, as in her earlier books, moves from the searching internal conversation of a poem like "Staircase" ("All of this/ Moving into me/ It will have to be enough") to the clear tone of a flawlessly realized lyric such as "Song at the Shore":

> Are not the rock-pools waiting
> To catch her questing face?
> Perhaps the sea, narrating
> Her story in this place?

Crone's Wines also includes a number of narrative poems, often ironic or tragicomic verse vignettes akin to Thomas Hardy's *Satires of Circumstance*. These tales, in which human foibles are revealed all too clearly, present an intriguing counterpart to the deeply hidden secrets, debts, and forgivenesses that are only hinted at glancingly in the first-person poems.

Although some of these poems are earlier poems that escaped inclusion in Maggie's previous books, most of them are late, and the volume's central theme is aging and, finally, death. The poems in the first section concern solitude and nature; the second, childhood memories and relatives; the third, remembered love; and the fourth, charmingly, cats. Most of these poems are in some way informed by the writer's age. The fifth section, *Sonnets to Hayes,* documents her passionate, if basically platonic, octogenarian love affair. The last section, perhaps my favorite, shines with the wisdom, lucidity and spiritual courage that I remember most about my mother as I look back on her life. These are the poems of the woman who devoured books about the Goddess and female-centered spirituality, purchased her favorite spiritual books in multiples to share with all her daughters, and always carried a slip of paper in her wallet on which she had copied out her current favorite inspirational quotation for meditation.

When the time came to put this book together, I gathered up Maggie's new poems and all the previously unpublished poems we could find, many of them collected and typed by the second of her four daughters, Marta Rijn Finch, who has been named Maggie's literary executor. I sat with Maggie in the spring of 2015 organizing and ordering them into what felt to me as cohesive sections with eloquent and moving arrangements. We decided to include light verse also, since it has long been part of Maggie's oeuvre (especially in later years when she was involved with the Maine Poets Society, where she served as copresident from 2007 to 2013 with Marta).

Though Maggie revised many of the poems in her earlier books repeatedly, the later poems in this book tend to have fewer revisions. In the interview below, she says that "the most important thing about writing poetry is that if you feel like writing it down you should write it down, otherwise you'll forget it." Based on the drafts I've seen, a good number of these poems seem to be gifts that came complete, with not much more needed but to write them down.

I showed Maggie each stage of this manuscript and asked for her input, and though her attention span was shortening by then and she wasn't able to make active creative decisions about the shape of the book, she happily approved the selection, final organization, and order of the poems. And during the process, she broke her lifelong pattern and actually accepted several (though not all!) of my small editorial suggestions, a great gift that made me feel she trusted me at last.

Annie Finch
Falmouth, Maine
April 20, 2016
(Maggie's ninety-fifth birthday)

Preface

Now that I am "of a certain age" (as it is so delicately put) and my daughter Annie has so generously offered me her time and effort in helping me prepare this (undoubtedly my last) book—at a time when she should only be interested in bringing out a book of her own poems—she has plunked a pen into my hand and instructed me, "Write a little preface."

So I am writing a little preface. A thing I have never been required to do before. So I'll be very green at it, and it might be better if you just stopped reading this right now!

I was fortunate enough to be brought up on a beach at Cape May Point, New Jersey, having been born in Bridgeton a year or so before. My mother took care of my three brothers (who required a lot of it) but was delighted to finally have the daughter she'd always longed for (her firstborn had also been a boy, who had lived less than a year).

She and I certainly got along famously from the get-go, as I was her "favorite gift" (and all my life I have felt very aware that I had been her best-ever birthday present—and none of my friends could match that!). My arrival (after her four sons) must have been all the sweeter since I came when my parents were recovering from a temporary break-up, caused by my father's ever-wandering heart (which he seemed unable to rein in, until he met his second wife, Esther Grayson).

When I was four years old I spoke a poem to my mother, which
she promptly wrote down, in order, I'm sure, to read it to her sisters,
Jessie and Evelyn Hughan. She was not all that interested in poetry
herself, but knew of course that Jessie would be especially delighted.
Their mother, a musician, had composed quite a few songs.

I started out modestly. This poem had only two lines:

> I come from the sun.

> I come to fly!

Maggie Finch
Portland, Maine
May 4, 2015

Interview with Maggie Finch

With Annie Finch

AF: So what happened after that first poem? Did you write poetry in elementary school, or in that Communist school you went to?

MRF: I don't remember whether I wrote poetry in elementary school … did I write poetry at Manumit School? I don't remember.

AF: What about with Mr. Stolper, in high school?

MRF: Yes. At Lincoln School there was Mr. Stolper. As I recall, we were taken to the museum and shown some old Egyptian vases or something, and then we got back to school and the teacher said, "write a poem about what you saw." So I wrote a poem, and I suppose that was the way it started. We were very close for a long time and I showed him all the poems I wrote. He was so interested in me and my future that he asked me if he could please come and have tea with my mother. He wanted to talk to her and make sure that she wasn't just some scrubwoman who had never read a poem. He wanted to find out my background because he wanted them to treat me properly as a developing poet. I remember he came to tea and of course my aunts Jessie and Evelyn would be there too, as they were very much involved because my mother and I lived alone—my father had long since departed. So they would be part of anything like that. And I remember that was quite exciting when Mr. Stolper came out to meet—poor man—my mother and my two aunts, all at once, you see. You can imagine. He was a very brave man, to come. He thought I had great possibilities. I'm sure he thought I was going to become a great poet or something.

AF: And did you?

MRF: No I didn't, Annie! I was too busy having you.

AF: You didn't because you had children?

MRF: Oh, you know. I was too busy falling in love, out of love . . .

AF: But that gave you something to write about.

MRF: It sure did!

AF: OK, keep going!

MRF: Where am I now?

AF: So after Mr. Stolper, then what?

MRF: Well, there really wasn't anyone after Mr. Stolper. When I graduated from Lincoln School and went on to college, I didn't have anyone at college that I showed poems to. I would just send them all in the mail to Stolper, and he would make comments on the poem and send it back to me, you know.

AF: You were reading Millay in college, right?

MRF: Oh, I was reading her I think long before college—let me see—I don't know how I got started on Millay . . . I'm trying to remember. You see, it might have been my friend Ania, who had started reading Millay and got all excited and lent me the books and so forth and so on, I don't remember. Because she wrote poetry too. But not as a poet, the way I was doing. She was my great—what would you say—my creative friend. She's the one who took me to the ballet . . .

AF: Did you want to be a poet at that time?

MRF: I don't really remember wanting to be a poet, you know. Maybe it would be more accurate to say I took it for granted that I was one, and was going to be one, rather than wanting to be one.

AF: Did you want to get published?

MRF: Oh, I imagine so. Let me see about that. Yes, I was sending out things to magazines and this and this.

AF: And you continued to do that.

MRF: Yes.

AF: You also wanted to be a sculptor and a dancer and an actress. Were those things less serious?

MRF: Those things were physical. It meant I had to practice and take lessons. Being a poet, you didn't have to do any exercises or anything, and I was always very physically lazy.

AF: Do you think that's why you became a poet—because you were lazy?

MRF: Well it certainly helped, didn't it?

AF: I guess so! Who would you say were your main influences?

MRF: Who were my influences! That's quite a question, Annie.

AF: Well, if you had to name five poets you admired, who would you say?

MRF: Five poets I admired at that time? Certainly Millay. I was crazy about her. And there was someone very similar to Millay. A woman, you know, about the same age, about the same fame. Who was that?

AF: Elinor Wylie?

MRF: I don't think I was ever that much into Elinor Wylie.

AF: Sarah Cleghorn?

MRF: Cleghorn? No. I won't say I was anti-Cleghorn, but I was a non-Cleghorn person, you know.

AF: Was it Teasdale?

MRF: Sara Teasdale!

AF: You liked her?

MRF: Oh, I think I did, yes. Teasdale. I think I was very fond of her.

AF: She's the one Marya [Zaturenska] worked on. I think you used to say you didn't like her so much.

MRF. Oh, yes. I liked Teasdale.

AF: So Millay and Teasdale. Any other poets that you liked?

MRF: Well, certainly not Horace Gregory [Gregory was Zaturenska's husband; they were family friends].

AF: Who are your favorite poets now?

MRF: Hmm . . . that's quite a question, isn't it!

AF: Hopkins? I know you love Hopkins . . .

MRF: Hopkins, yes . . .

AF: What do you think is the most important thing about writing poetry?

MRF: The most important thing about writing poetry? Annie, please! The most important thing about writing poetry is that if you feel like writing it down you should write it down, otherwise you'll forget it.

AF: What makes a good poem, do you think?

MRF: I have no idea!

AF: How did you write them?

MRF: With a pencil. Or with a pen.

ALLEGRO: Meow!

MRF: Oh, I didn't know you wrote them. I thought I wrote them. Now he tells me! Annie, write that down. Actually Allegro wrote all the poems. Allegro wrote them all. [To Allegro] Didn't you darling, yes. But you let me take the credit. You knew they'd never believe you if you said you wrote them. [Looking at the manuscript] Gee, there are a lot of them, Annie. How many did I write? I wrote a lot, didn't I?

AF: Yes you did! A lot. And they are wonderful.

MRF: Do you honestly think any of them are any good?

AF: Oh, yes, I really do!

MRF: (smiling) That's wonderful!

AF: So I'm trying to ask you some of the questions people might want to know. When you write, does the whole thing come into your mind, or just a line, or does it vary?

MRF: One line at a time I would say—or one phrase at a time, I would say. Or sometimes you think of a line and you think that's wonderful and you try to write the next two or three and it doesn't work, so you have to throw out that first great line, and you get nowhere with it. You know that.

AF: Umm, no . . . I would never throw out the first great line.

MRF: No, I'm not saying throw it out, but, you know, set it aside for a different poem.

AF: I would just keep the great line I think.

MRF: Well . . .

AF: Anyway . . . is there anything else you want to say about your poetry?

MRF: I wish I were writing more of it now, I'll tell you . . . !

AF: Well, maybe publishing this book will get you started!

MRF: Maybe. I do hope so!

Contents

Voices over Water

Go, Gather Shells

That We May Share

Sonnets to Hayes

The Cat's Dinner

Crone's Wines

Crone's Wines

Voices over Water

Another Perspective

(at an antique window)

A leaf falls from
My venerable tree—
Small and yellow, falling
Into this my autumn,

But my catching breath discovers
Another's autumn lost and long
Ago, the curtain caught aback
From open window by—whose hand?

Hers—not mine, where she leans
Watching, waiting, her young tree
Inside my old tree she uncovers
Where my air trembles through her leaves—

One is small and yellow, falling
Through the air not mine but hers.

Will, one day, another woman find me
Leaning, waiting—and wonder in a breath
Who this may be, her hand upon the curtain,
Through watching autumn tree, not hers but mine?

After News of a Massacre, 2007

At dawn of storm a gull
Blown inland from the sea
Seeks impossible lull,
Circles my greatest tree.
Her cries come, chronicle
Steeped in our misery.

At my high window, caught
In worlds of twisted pride
(Unnatural deaths, dear bought
In agonies) I hide
But cannot.

Now—my thought
To call her safe inside:

I fling my casement wide.

The Springing Sun

Lint-worn I walk the weathered field
To feel the springing sun
Come on my shoulders, as it healed
My forebears, every one

(And as it heals my children now
And will their children, too).
What, save the sun, can disallow
Dark and the cold night-dew?

Surrounded by those trivial fires
That die, not to return,
I have come here where all desires
Lack substance, lack concern.

Why do I search the creeds they had
To warm them through the years?
For all are gone, who winter-clad
Crossed the wide river's tears—

And some held faith, and some grew slack,
And none could prove it so—
And feeling sun upon my back
Is all I need to know.

Voices over Water

Voices of strangers coming over water
However haunting, do not, cannot stay;
Even though understood, the moving water
Carries the words of strangers, lost, away.

Voices that love us coming over water,
However faint and far, however fleet,
Bring a bright singing over lovely water:
Words laid on the heart, that help it beat.

Voices we loved over remembered water
However gone, echo like childhood song
Whispering down the body's living water
Where words they told us, murmur in us, lifelong.

Staircase

What does it say to me?
Light that comes through
The west window
At four, at five
Of the good clock,
Stroking the white spokes
(They go up and down)

Dark steps going up,
White spokes coming down?

Are they too quiet?

Do they say softly it will be enough—
All of this
Moving into me
It will have to be enough—

I tell them, say
Out loud
So they can hear

I'm listening, I'm listening,
I'm here and listening,
Just tell me, tell me,

Dark steps going down.

Open Doors

Still
I have not
Quite been able to express
What it *is*—about them—
Especially when—early
They begin to gather
Light

Their stillness more still than walls waking they say
(Whispering)—*What shall we do today?*
What shall we do with this gift of day?

Their splendid uprightness reaching upward always
Where ceilings carve those perfect corners into praise.

And knobs of open doors, don't they
Say—No need to turn
Me or even knock, just come straight in
(Smiling) I have no secrets—?

Or is it simply
Because the doors
Might be
Closed?
(But are not?)

Inlet, Tidal River at Flood

The tree in the air, the tree in the water
Joined above earth, below the air:
Trunk unto trunk within the water
Where no breath troubles the air,

Where no breath troubles the still
Essence of tree extending tree:
So—let me mirror this moment still:
Be metaphor of mirror-tree.

In October

Now my tall trees
Give in, discuss with wind
How leaves should heed the call,

And among these
The lofty oak, chagrined,
Though noisiest of all

Finally agrees
(Though prematurely thinned)
To clustered overhaul:

But, as if to tease,
Or prove self-disciplined,
Saves some singles for the last snowfall.

At Moosehead

Our moon beyond the hill
Already set—
Our sun across the lake
Not risen yet—
Stars hidden by dark trees
(Or—they forget)—

Now—when the earth is still—
Caught in its net
Of sleep—(nothing can make
The smallest threat)—

Might not angels, at their ease,
Forgive our debt?

Dawn over the Kennebec

A brief, a scarlet bird
Rises to stretch and hover
Uttering songs unheard
(Sweeter than sweetest lover).

Over the water's Yes
(Reflection's other name)—
Perhaps today's caress
Will stay, will stay the same.

Now—even as wings depart—
Rose, on the breast of river,
Offers its petaled heart
(The ultimate forgiver).

On the Various Levels of Pleasure

When sweet silk follows after rag,
Or saintly scholar after scalawag,
It does behoove us—in our newfound cheer—
To speak out: grateful, adamant, sincere:
Praising the Goddess—oh, my goodness—yes!
For her Divine Largesse . . .
Yet—not forgetting that the meager day
Served—in its humble way.

For the downcast
Partake of pleasures utterly unsurpassed,
On late arrival in the stratosphere.
Hardly believing what is clear
(Wrapped in the question, "Am I really here?")

Who better can enjoy what truly matters,
Than one who suffered through a life in tatters?

March Waking

Some very rising Bach
(Approaching opening)
One of them ushers in
Through mullioned morning lights the quivering lights of river.

Do I imagine only
(Only imagining)
On first blush,
Whisper of green along my drowsy pear tree twigs?

Both (untouching) cats
As if on well-known signal
Stretch to their ultimate claws
Slipping back into gathered sleep all (silent-spoken) once.

What could be quieter?
Now someone's Water Music
Gently rows my boat
Head letting it (so downstream) for the dream of waking.

Therefore, Come

Let me give you, this morning
(Quiet morning on the quiet river)
Five untroubled goldeneyes
Close to shore
Advancing without ripple . . . without wake . . .
And three poking
Laggards.

Feathered flotilla:
Serenity of eight ducks.

(Today's, tomorrow's, distant ends—
How many countless thunderings?—
Agonies of acrid, twisted acres
Tear at the human heart.)

Therefore, come and watch,
Breath in
At least this humble progress:

These small pieces of silent life
Laving the water, the air:

Especially, somehow,
The laggards.

Anniversary

Born in these trees
Born at this window
where pacing
Born in this room
where blue's bolt
Rearranged things invisible
to the eye

Born in this body on the verge

And the trees still they stand
Peering in, withholding comment
except when wind makes the move
Her faithful window
closes out what should be

As for room he continues
in the nature of rooms
to assert continuity:
Bed, bureau, chair

And the body

Waiting

Cross Country

I'm traveling, I'm traveling, I'm traveling
Away from you, who said you were
My lover—
(Here I am, not knowing the names of birds
Over somebody's field)

Traveling to a person's laughter
(That's where the future lies).
You, too, could find me amusing.
You, too, could find me amazing.

I've heard that corner crops
Feel less loved, and do not do so well,
But then, I have to wonder—
Who loves this tumult of rioting sumac beside the tracks?

Just after sunrise
I'm so intimate with leaves,
So fortunate to meet
This unassuming road
Trotting beside slowed train
Like an elderly dog
That understands one's moods.

Now, acres of corn in remarkable rows
Even over hills, even around old trees
That won out: would you believe
Every thriving row is aimed
At my passing window?
How did the farmers all know
I'd be by?

Ringwood Valley

The afternoon is lonely as a bird
Pushing the air: each attitude is cold
And deep as any wind, as snow hills old.
Fear forms within the word.

Evening lies beyond the shiver tree
Unpeopled, filled with absence, where the white
Grows ever quieter in failing light
Where loneliness and cold together see,

Together hear, a lone dog running bark
At no stranger and at no actual thing:

Then night will come, then night will come, and bring
A brimming silence filling up the dark.

A Vernal Query

Tag ends of snow, and tenderness
Of early willow-show
Brought tremolos of birds, to bless
The middle-ground of slow . . .

Or—did birds bring this warming glow
When they arrived to sing
To cold trees standing comfortless
Awaiting their redress,
Wanting to grow—and did both bring
At last, reverse of snow?

Traveler's Song

23

Leave early in the mind,
Leave early in the body:
Soon or late we grieve:

While the new voice is kind
And tells a likely story
Be wise: do not believe:

Ribbons of tongue will bind
Our little feet so easy:
It is too late to leave

When joy has made us blind,
And grief will have us early
Within the net we weave.

Learning from Early Coffee

Drinking the first one on a winter day,
Wrap the cup carefully with all your fingers,
If you would like to learn a little lesson:

(Or tea will do—the better, some would say).
Then, notice how the outer warmth still lingers,
Comforting—though the inner comforts lessen.

Observe the Butterfly

Observe the butterfly that sits the flower
With soft swaying; follow the box-
Turtle through thicket; the toad creep after;
Pause, intrigued, to notice how
The ant is terrible with delicate power;
Consider river's handling of rocks
And watch a spider dropping down from rafter.

Where is your self-preoccupation now?

Kennebec: Catching the Eastern Shore

Each late-lit afternoon
My Goddess of the Sun
Come to lie in longing arms—
At last the prize won:

But quick—the prize lost!
Always so briefly spun—
This joy of her compassionate form
In gold comparison.

All soon, the river crossed
She goes to lie in the west:
There—brief-lingering—she dies
In dazzling fires dressed . . .

Yet valued more—this blaze!
All radiance is outdone
Here where gone—so sudden—kills
A glory just begun.

Meander Path

Comes night—light lost—bitterness found,
Where to our cost
We lose our ground
And compass, in the blinding dark, storm-tossed:

Comes day—light found—
Bitterness lost,

We climb the mound
And trace, embossed,
Courageous patterns where our path has wound.

Country Song

Let the mouse
Come in my house,
Let her play fast and loose
And even reproduce—
(If she can find a spouse)
But—not in my favorite blouse!

Here is spider
Who, insider her,
Totes an efficient ladder—
Not being—the least—a gadder.
Well done, courageous glider!
Oh!—flies? I'll be provider.

Even ant,
Though adamant
And, yes, impertinent
When means of nourishment
Appear, provides a slant
On charm that others can't.

So, creatures, come:
I can accommodate some.

But not too many.
(Hardly any.)

To Mr. W.S. Merwin,
On Reading "To This May"

Over and over, bringing my birthday
(That is a day that brings a birth of light)
You ply your vision so that I might play.

Brought by a friend upon the first of May,
These hidden words send out a bird in flight
Over and over, bringing my birthday.

In language where all quietnesses stay,
Moving and blending colors come into white,
You ply your visions so that I might play.

Its light pretending not to move, you say,
Revealing the unutterable sight
Over and over, bringing my birthday.

Convincing me that in some secret way
I am the one you love and when you write
You ply your vision so that I might play.

How gratefully I fall beneath your sway!
You lead me to the land where all unite
Over and over, bringing my birthday,
You ply your vision, so that I might play.

Go, Gather Shells

Go, Gather Shells

This is for Peggy, here, inside, somewhere.
Put back together earliest of joys,
Old Jersey pleasures from forgotten air;
Five loves forever true; creation's toys;
The games of waves; box turtle on the floor
Eating her tomato; garden shed
Miraculously turn playhouse, with a door
Of favored green; a new doll in her bed
Under a Christmas tree

All in your reach
Almost, sometimes . . . yet there is none to say,
Remember tide pools in the front yard beach,
Their king crabs?"

Childhood's Child

Father's farm, father's farm:
Though he was strong
Laboring sweet and long
With his right arm:

Lost, lost his loving charm.
Oh, it was wrong!—
Still cries the undersong,
Harvesting harm.

Coward, Coward

Better than this—the revealing hour,
Better the world that should be spoken
As spreading web by rock is broken:
Taut, tremulous threads meeting a stone's power.

But coward, coward, blind and frail the heart
Muttering to itself, refusing to yield
To possibility the fear it holds apart:
Lone figure—crying—crossing a lonely field.

The Lost Garden

Earliest of all doorways, and the old
Porches of childhood—when I pull them back
Even the tender bleeding-hearts unfold
Only in outline for they oddly lack
Recollection of color, scent and shape—
As rose, as daffodil I know were there.
How can that lovely tapestry escape
Without a trace, faded from former air?

Called to mind: those low rock walls by the sea,
Steep stone steps down to lawn, the ardent green
Of alien bamboo; an arbor's plea
For bud and blossom (but no vine is seen)
Unfinished vision: all that I can know:
Gardener's garden where no flowers grow.

Althea's Cinderella

Well, this girl, this girl,
She liked to live in the fireplace and sweep it
Only they made her do it
But she liked to do it
And her mother was somebody else
And her sisters weren't real sisters

And then—and then—
There was a ball at the palace with all the candles
And that's when people dance and
They were mean and said she couldn't go
But this fairy came with a wand and a star at the end
(But I think it was really her mother who died)
Well—well—she just hit the pumpkins and mice and things, well, they
Turned into a—like a wagon with a roof and horses and a new dress
(Because she did that with her magic wand, see)
And she went over there so she could dance and sweep out their fireplace
But there was a Prince and he liked her little slipper all made of glass
In the middle of the night a lot and looked for the other one she lost

And then—and then—he came to her house and found it on her foot
Even if they were mean and they got married—(isn't that a great story?)

About That Widow

It was, perhaps, the measure of her grief,
If we believe the show was genuine.
One must assume reality—if brief—

Yet—with a modicum of disbelief.
In any marriage, there is thick-and-thin:
It was, perhaps, the measure of her grief.

His charm was shallow as a bas-relief;
We're told his childhood was the origin:
One must assume reality, if brief.

Once, he was called a veritable thief;
Though never caught (to many folks' chagrin),
It was, perhaps, the measure of her grief.

In any drinking party, he was chief:
(Back home, a nasty kick would make her spin . . .
One must assume reality—if brief).

But: had she never read the interleaf?
Nor loved the vulnerable boy within?
It was, perhaps the measure of her grief.
(One must assume reality—if brief.)

Old Mags

Old clockwork Mags, we called her—and it worked
For mocking one so muddled—but, unknown,
Within the gray, a burnished lifetime lurked.

Behind our hands we laughed at her and smirked,
But in her hands a measured world had grown.
Old clockwork Mags, we called her—and it worked

For one who, seeing duty, had not shirked.
Why didn't we respect the undertone?
Within the gray, a burnished lifetime lurked.

Single, supporting children, she had clerked
In shops where patrons asked for her alone.
Old clockwork Mags, we called her—and it worked

Through all those hectic days: the coffee perked,
Times-tables faltered, and all rips were sewn.
Within the gray, a burnished lifetime lurked

And, sorely tempted, she was seldom irked
Even in age, equable to the bone.
Old clockwork Mags, we called her—and it worked:
Within the gray, a burnished lifetime lurked.

Neatly Done

She sang her sister childhood songs, toward end,
And fed her with a favorite spoon from home;
Read parts of letters from their failing friend,
Snippets from a loved and cheerful tone.
She brought the hand-washed pillowslips their mother
Had embroidered for a happier day
Which never came: not that one, nor another.
And now the years crept on, slow roundelay.

Two prayers she prayed: Let me not die before;
And when I do, let me not linger long . . .
Her sister died. Then, gods were keeping score!
She dropped and died one day, though seeming strong.

I like to think of justice neatly done:
For one good woman, one good benison.

My Cousin

In an old list torn at the edges
I find the worlds write Lee
And I cannot remember
Whether I did. Probably not.

When I was lost and little
I found my mother crying:
"Aunt Edna is dead
And I never answered her last letter."

Dear, dear Lee,
Recounter of gentle gossip,
Reader of Murasaki,
Embroiderer of flowers,

Woman of resolution

Have you forgiven me, you

Who—later—wrote to tell me
You were leaving—

No—
Who wrote to tell me
(Asking forgiveness)
You were already dead.

Lines for Morag Aitkenhead

Lois has told me of the horse and cart,
Beloved Morag. Would that I could go
Walking behind with footsteps sad and slow—
Woman who walked, one day, into my heart—

Never to leave. Tomorrow I will mark
My hours to weave your clock, imagining
The gentle progress—and, remembering
You who held—always—the angelic spark.

I sit beside the river and, above,
Gulls wheel and cry as if, somehow, they knew:
The passing of a spirit, wise, where grew
Compassion's shining flower, wreathed in love.

Great-Uncle John

Mornings, I stir my coffee with your spoon.
Not a single morning comes or goes
But contemplation of this little boon
Wishes silent silver could disclose
The man behind the flourished monogram.
At seventeen you left the family farm,
Entered importing. Sturdy, without sham,
You flourished there—but lacked, they said, all charm
And found no wife.

Solemnity of mien,
Approaching frown: your photo hits the mark.
From paucity of stories we can glean
One fading star against encroaching dark:
The favorite niece, so curiously endeared
By fabled bracelet—long since disappeared.

Bronzino's Eleonora of Toledo with
Her Son, Don Giovanni

Sauntering past their corner of the room,
Enquire: Is this a portrait of a dress?
After three hundred years her opened tomb
Tells what Bronzino saw, and answers: Yes.
The same brocaded bones of wedding day—
Young bride, young death. Duchess de Medici.

Perhaps no pearl-sewn silk, wrapping her fragile clay,
Could fend the joys of infidelity
After eleven heirs for Cosimo.

She took a villa, patronized—not Arts
(Tuscany's Duck fast in his Vecchio)—
But artists, Jesuits, poets . . . counterparts
Who loved and honored what Bronzino caught
Beneath the velvet breast of chatelaine.
For there is wisdom that is dearly bought.
A stone for bread. Look in her eyes again.
They say there was a cherished painter-priest,
One Alessandro. Though we know his name:
Pandolfo: yet the rest is rumor's feast.
("Malaria"—not assassin—was the claim.)

On the Twentieth of April

The morning of our natal days
Rises again, so sweet and mild
As does befit our ever-ways—
You, the mother—I, the child.

Recalling how we always strove
To share at least a part of it
I give this dawning to our love
(The earliest, the heart of it),

This day when you, between your bites
Of festive cake, brought into birth
My happy self, who so delights
In having walked upon your earth

So many years—and now believes
That it will come, the wish that's nearest:
To know again, the love that weaves
Such joy, O mother, you the dearest!

Lynne's Gifts

Aunt Lynne visited seldom, living far,
Yet always when she came
Brought saved-up gifts that filled her little car,
Winning our warm acclaim.

She'd lost her heart, but to a taken man
Who would not leave his mate
(Though he was smitten, too) and thus began
Their dance of sit-and-wait.

"With love like ours," she'd say, "no matter, age!
For we are in God's hand.
Perhaps, some day, I'll move to center stage
And wear his wedding band.

Meanwhile, I save up gifts—of every kind,
To pleasure him—at last."

And so she dreamed, watching the clock unwind,
Adoring and steadfast.

Then—what?—A miracle, as some might say,
His wife, at forty-seven,
In perfect health, astonished all, one day:
She tripped, and went to heaven.

At last, at last, Lynne hurried to prepare:
A prudent date was set,
The church reserved . . . the answer to her prayer
Wrapped up in etiquette.

But from the heights, alas, she was cut down.
Too soon, before she'd shaken
The creases from her mother's heirloom gown,
Her sweetheart's life was taken.

For years his memory cradled her hope chest—
Locked, where we could not see—
Until she died, his picture on her breast.
We never found the key

Her saved-up gifts, we knew, were never given,
Her favor never sought:
We knew that Lynne had safely died—unshriven—
(Or so, at least, we thought.)

The Disappeared

(for the grandmothers of the Plaza de Mayo)

Who are you—were you—where and when?
Might this hand bring you back again?

Fetching horses, were you revealed
Careless in the family field

Or running at dawn along the shore?
(Footsteps found, not found before.)

It could be: hanging out the clothes—
The child at play—the threats, the blows—

Or huddled in locked cellar bed:
Hearing a creak above your head.

Perhaps—two, walking in the wood,
Great trees sheltering as they could—

(Yes! Love, lying under the stars,
Guarded by Venus—and by Mars?)

Who tries to slip into the crowd,
Praying not to be disallowed?

Or hides, with an insistent cough,
Waiting for soldiers to move off? . . .

Listen! Do you drift back in view?
Whether or not: I mourn for you.

A Candle in the Small Hours

(at Gary and Dabney's house)

Outside, the horses sleep, waiting under
California's moon; here—the house waits
Sleeping, apparently. And yet—a wonder
Grows as I pause—for stillness dedicates
A deeper stillness to all wood, all weaving,
Careful things all, ingathered by wise hands—
Left quiet, candlelit, within our leaving:
Each chair, each table, free of our demands.

Now, "Anahita's Horses of the Dawn"
Plunge marble-live off shadowy wall; and blooms
Rising from rich rugs colored like a lawn
Called flowers, beckon, dim, from distant looms.

I stand bemused: the house a life of art:
Cupped and glowing, like the candle-heart.

The Misplaced Poem

(for Annie)

It did concern your head, bobbing above
The line of dying hedges in the fall
As you set off, tugging against my love,
That first-grade year—alone. You'd slipped the caul.
I stood on the back porch to watch you go
And waved, as, turning, you reached neighbor's rise
And disappeared. You were a cameo
Of eager confidence. My inner eyes
Beheld you whole,
In it there was a crown . . .
Within a crown? You questioned me, years back,
As I remember, with your wisp of frown.
Maybe that's why it hid—down some fond crack:
Those treasured lines, that saw before I knew.
They were about the Annie-ness of you.

Tutankhamun

I.
Why do I think of the boy-king in his tomb?
Not dream, but ponder carefully, so deep
The centuries of slow-paced ever-gloom
Wrap his limbs where the immortals keep . . .
Why do I muse on the dry years drifting down
Over the useless air, whose dark belie
(Over the turns of linen turning brown
Under unchanging gold) the ceaseless eye
Doubled in stare?
Oh, why consider—why?—
His funeral bones of birds, the broom beside
That sweeps him down to death and up to sky
Where faults and charities no longer hide,
And all is readiness to discover whether
His young heart will outweigh the Fatal Feather.

II.
How did he reach the stone steps cut in doom?
Blow-damaged skull—after the early crowning—
(Which was the god that chose him in the womb?)—
Perhaps too many priests and nobles frowning
And whispering together, unhappy still
Though he had moved the throne to Thebes again.
And changed his name? They not content until
He was safe in solid gold? We ask, but no staunch pen
Glyphed the day's moments. Here, the bed of lion,
Sweet chairs—gods, slaves attending—food and treasure—
Even, perhaps, the longed-for, stillborn scion
(For babe there is)—all life—all death—good measure:
Yet Carter's astonished flashlight could not hear
The words forever lost—however near.

Three Ships

There was a woman by the sea
(With a heigh, with a ho)
Lived in a tower with windows three
(With a heigh-ho)

She hung a lantern in each light
(With a heigh, with a ho)
To guide her good ships home at night
(With a heigh-ho).

I sent three ships across the wave
(With a heigh, with a ho)
But others' treasures they did crave
(With a heigh-ho)

We'll have each treasure-laden barque
(With a heigh, with a ho)
No lights to guide them through the dark
(With a heigh-ho),

And down they went, and paid the fee
(With a heigh, with a ho)—
And lost the treasures meant for me.

That We May Share

Triad

First, the roof:
Shelter of house above
Storm's bed where I had lain
Counting the cost of love—
(And your voice in the rain).

Then, the fire
No longer burning cruel
Gently revealed your name:
I knew who brought the fuel—
(And your face in the flame).

Now, the food:
Simple as loaf in hand
Whereby the flesh is fed
To feed the soul's demand—
(Our bodies in the bread).

Whether or Not

Whether or not the hand is taken,
Whether or not the promise made,
Comes an earlier faith forsaken,
Earlier trust again betrayed:
Vulnerable as rose wind-shaken
Hangs the heart—alone, afraid.

Whether or not the kiss is given
Where warm embrace is easy-got,
Over and over we are driven
Into the fearful cold—the what
And where, long since, as heart was riven:
Though the mind remembers not.

You Are Appointed to Everlasting Glory

Voice that I long to hear
Come out of the clouds
Low-lying, heavy with things hard to breathe.

All they give me is
Tie my shoestring please
What time does the kitchen clock say?

It doesn't say to me
It never will, it can't
You know I'm stone deaf.

Why do you tease?
When will clouds lift?
Have you heard the chime or seen the hands move?

Yes, I'm blind, too.
I wasn't going to tell you
But when I hear the voice the scales will fall—

They always do
I know they always do
They go to pave the awful way to hell

Something has to go
To pave the awful way, well something must
Because it's there and it must be gotten to

But when I hear the voice
And scales fall and clocks chime and the clouds
Leave my lungs I will be tying latchets

And breathing easy
Way over the sparkling stones to hell
Hear every clock say everything I long to hear.

Find One

I wear two bracelets, as you see,
Upon my wrinkled wrist,
And both of them are part of me—
And both of them were kissed.

The first is gold, though very thin,
The second, silver pure.
See, one of them can fit within
The other's aperture.

Which one, think you, betokens laughter
Never to be my sup?
(That fatal look: forever:
The kiss left in the cup.)

The other love was new this round,
But—just as mandatory.
It spelled a happiness profound
And told a different story.

Please, listen . . . At my final sleep
Make of deep hope a tether:
Find one who promises to keep
Silver and gold together.

Out of Silence

Into the dark I travel, where
An old tree leans against a star
And, silently, a small stream there
Goes glimmering still (where no sounds are)—

Goes glimmering the name called lover
Out of silence, out of dismal day
(There, where death could not discover
Where we two, undying, lay).

Into the dark I travel, hear
Sounds—as someone overtaking:
Are your footsteps hurrying near?
Or—is that my own heart breaking?

Left

The shape of my sleeves
deep in his looking glass
could do for me
(hear how they grieve).

Flipped collar claims
we're here, see
and we are all for you,
we make the best of you.

Just feel the sweetness
of our brocade!

Body, it's called,
hand, it's called—

But, honestly, it is these shapes of shadows
long and longing out from the off-white boards
building darkening walls
as darkness falls—

Cradle my head, take me—
take me.

The Wind

I called it wind because the wind was loud:
Louder than ever, rattling to get in
Wherever it was out—and it was proud
To have arrived, determined it would win:
This love I call the wind. Beside the Bay
We drank our tea, offered analyses
Concerning sudden weather, the strange way
It modeled water, shook the ancient trees . . .

What else—beside the master of old waves
Returned from early beaches—mythic Sea
Storming the nights, digging our father's graves—
Could grapple us to breast: could captor be?

We loved the wind. Alas, we did not know
That day, that it would never let us go.

Your Silence

My dear, you are wrapped, still in a question mark
Of sighs, of listening: your care was cruel
Longer than it was kind, as though a dark
And shadowed setting held a hidden jewel;
As though the flowers you brought me were mirage

And bloomed under the breath of stars, to fade
As I awoke—where wordless camouflage
Denied a hollow promise never made.

And yet, the good is here: all that you gave
Unstintingly to one so much in need . . .
Perhaps your silence, reaching from the grave,
Teaches a final lesson to my greed:

I'm ready, now, to quit the pain of charting
The riddles of our love—and of our parting.

For a Time

Sometimes I lose your face, and I must look
At the old image taken long ago
Before you left the party and forsook
For good or ill, the only world we know.
Sometimes the memory of your brow
Furrowed in thought, escapes me for a time,
Or I am ignorant, alas, of how
Your eyes, expressive as a pantomime,
Spoke sweetly, or enquired.

So, then, I find
Your photograph (fixed grays against the white),
Forgetting that my heart grows old and blind,
Hoping to bring you back into the light:
I hold the frame: only to realize:
Here is the face, it whispers—but it lies.

That We May Share

If you came early, you would see the leaves
Hang yellow, here, and red, as has been told:
Melange of scarlet-saffron that achieves
A glory (made with) counterpoints of gold.
Cacophonies from trees, high in the tops,
Explode: perhaps crows want their branches free
Without the wait for wind (shaking, as drops
Of sun-filled water down, a shower). Listen to me.
If you come late, dun leaves will play and spin
Low on the ground: how will they please you then?—
(As all the whites of winter settle in
To silence crows and colors once again).
Come soon, my dear, that we may share this scene:
This dying flame, this perfect go-between.

Anonyme

Do not ask after me:
Like bird in summer leaves,
So I in autumn tree
Shadow my self, go free
Where I make mystery:
One among many thieves—
And there my heart will be.

I whisper my name, a guide
That only interweaves
To disconcert, divide
From any truth inside,
For I have only lied
To any who believes—
And there my love will hide.

So It May

As gradually as light over the hill
Springs love, when first it ventures to begin—
Or so it may—all tentative—until
Tenderly as approaching mandolin
Heralding a dawn to celebrate,
The tune unfolds, small notes grow full and clear,
And blessed is one who need no longer wait
In silent dark, but sees the sun appear.

Gentle affections carried in the hand
Like apples for the hungry: these can start
A view of orchards in a wonderland
Beyond the farthest reaches of the heart,
And every step along the astonished way
Deepens joy, day after quiet day.

Brave the Break

Don't ever phone to say, "Goodbye."
Further winds of abandon blow
Along these modern webs of sky
(Where only birds were meant to go).

Through centuries past, the humble pen
Has served to send, in desperate seasons,
The death of love—by women, men,
However far—whatever reasons.

True, neat or scribbled, marks on page
(No matter woven with regret)
Could wound, crush—cold—engender rage:
Heart-rending lines of flatness. Yet:

Warm hands had dipped and pushed the quill.
The natural had been nudged or flicked
(Human body shone human still:
Nerves tended wax . . . stamp had been licked).

Now—metal, plastic, wire and air
Leave us with—nothing you have held
Or even touched—nothing you care
To send—save fading words dispelled

Beneath the bridges . . . Always, make,
Where possible, the better choice
And that is: person. Brave the break,
And bring real face, and bring real voice.

But, oh, my lovers! Listen well!
Avoid the cruelest path of all:
The sudden cut that can not tell:
Silence—the blind, the bitter, wall.

Strange Things Blues

Walked in the door, caught him with a stranger,
Strange thing is—I never did feel stronger:
Now I knew that I could not stay there longer.

Walked out the door. I did not hesitate.
Strange thing is—I knew that I would forget.
Bury it deep, travel without regret.

Slammed the door shut, existing so grandly!
Strange thing is—left all my clothes behind me,
Came far away, so he'd never find me.

Stayed far away, so I'd never waver.
Strange thing is—I never did recover.
Day into night, hanker for that lover.

One of Us

Now, hearing my world wake
I know that I wake, too,
And wonder if you take
Your world inside of you.

Here, opening my eyes
In sweet for granted time,
I start to formalize
For us, a rightful rhyme.

As half-true love's viceroy
I labor to set down
(Deeper affection's ploy)
The pleasures of this crown:

The lessons of the past,
The tolerance of age:
Good sound of anchor cast
In evening harborage;

Compassion, silver-haired . . .
But, just before the lines
On mellow laughter shared—
Alas!—there intertwines

Longing for long delay
In kind adagio—
Since one of us must stay
When one of us must go.

The Haiku

Moon, riding . . . west,
did he send you to inquire
whether I lie late?

The Cinquain

I feel
March breezes touch
My face with April and I wonder how wind
found its way
from you.

The Understudy

His Lady was Philosophy: he loved
Her glance of wisdom. In her proud hands, gloved
In purity, he laid his ardent heart.
It was to her he sang, "Till death us part!"
Yes, I was understudy in that play,
(Though hardly suited, with my feet of clay):
How speak in dialogue with such a one,
Whose mistress was the Goddess of the Sun?

But, later (when, brought low, he needed me)
I stepped upon the stage most willingly:
He woke, I woke, and when he slept, I slept:
(My exits and my entrances well kept).

There came a night he fell upon the floor
And I the only one, however poor,
To lift him up: through love, through will, through prayer.
At last he heard my quiet lines. Oh, where
Was his fine Lady then, in her robes of white,
Girdled in gold, crowned in a Sea of Light?

It was to me he turned, in deep review,
And softly said, "Thank you for all you do."

Inheritor

Whoever you are, who gave me
A mind to hold belief,
A body strong as stone
And nerves sound as a bell—

My gratitude is deep.

But who, most of all, to save me
Brought heart for joy and grief—
Loving close to the bone,
Not wisely, but too well—

Yours, I will hope to keep.

Into the Winter

She is a springtime love, that nothing wants
Save to emerge and grow for her own sake,

Finding good days for giving as she hunts
For air to clothe her and for rain to slake
Temperate thirst. But mostly it is sun
I think she hankers for, just to exist
Upon an earth warmed by that Singleton
Without desire: by presence to be kissed.
It is a wonderment, how spring should fall
Into the winter of these edging days
Allotted us—her buds as wherewithal
For sweet commands, that nothing disobeys.

Even knowledge of storms cannot efface
The blossoming of this encounter's grace.

After Seven Years

Give me no silks from China, very dear,
Rainbow-colored, pearled, for me to wear.
Sandals of golden leather bring me not,
Their buckles bearing emeralds, nor yet
Do I require a silver diadem
Set with a ruby carrying a name:
Nor even that commended little hoop
Carbon-centered, burdened with such hope.

Skip coach and four decked all about in gold
To trance me to castle in a field
Of magic flowers, where a clutch of fairies
Lift willing hands . . . think of whatever marries
Wish a fond extreme . . . I will have none.
Were I to dream, I'd end where I began
In happiest of circles, for I crave
Only that single treasure I now have.

Since yesterday, I have been queen of all:
Upon my ears four simple syllables fell:
Your words admitting our platonic mating.
(That I was yours, I knew at our first meeting.)

The Door Ajar

Some words, though simple, leave the door ajar
That one may see, what vistas lie ahead.
"Thank you for being when and where you are."

Nine sounds were uttered, and dispelled the bar
Of reticence, and left the spirit fed.
Some words, though simple, leave the door ajar

But these, so quiet, cannot mean, bizarre,
"You have become my water and my bread."
Thank you for being when and where you are.

And now I say: You are a pilot-star
Who always leads me where I would be led—
Some words, though simple, leave the door ajar.

Were we not blessed, in coming from afar?
I can't remember which of us first said,
"Thank you for being when and where you are."

If I should meet, in his four-steeded car,
Apollo, I would smile at you instead!
Some words, though simple, leave the door ajar:
Thank you for being when and where you are.

Into the Clearing

What gift can I give him
To whom I would give all?
Not the daisy nodding by the water's edge,
Not the chatter of swallows amiable and small
Nor their silent flight
Bringing a straw . . .
Could I send the taste of strawberries
Warm, sweet from the sun?
The scent of my single rose, opening this morning?

None of these. None of these.

But I can send him words
Where in the dark we walk,
Where in the forest he walks:

My true love, take the light
Of all my care
And use it as you will
And leave me if your life
Needs leaving me—
Leave me if your path
Could thus be found.

See, I bring the lantern of my heart
And take your hand
And lead you from me
Into the clearing—
Into the clearing
Though it be empty of me . . .
Oh, my love.

What Think You?

There is a bowl I have in mind to build,
The workmanship so fine
That half the beauty of the world, distilled,
Could lie in it, like wine.

I'd study how to make, with master hand,
The whole, from base to rim,
... And gather carefully from every land
The structure, as wherewithal means for ground and trim.

Silver and gold, the best, would be a start:
... jewels, vivid, shining,
Set in, to work a message from my heart:
Clear crystal for the lining ...

Little flowering landscapes would enhance
The rising sides all round:
Two handles shaped like goddesses in dance
Hearing a lovely sound ...

What think you?—But, alas, I am too old
To fashion the above.
So take, I pray, these lines, that your mind may hold
The image of my love.

Sonnets to Hayes

In Reply to "A Poem for Maggie"

Parents, husbands, lovers, children, friends,
Over the years, have sent me Valentines—
Most in affection (some to make amends)—
A few, of course, were merely countersigns.

When I look back upon the decades flown,
Some messages seemed fine, some made me cry,
And some—so shamelessly—were overblown!
At last, comes one that cannot falsify.

Today, arrived the best I can recall:
Though I am wrinkled, of a certain age,

Your lines, my darling, are dearest of them all,
For, "blood and sweat and tears run down the page!"

Better Late than Never

Even if I should have a valentine
"Hanging around somewhere,"
(Perhaps produced for some lad who was mine
Whom I thought, naturally, the very best)

I would not stoop to falsity and tender
To you the burning words meant for a day
Long since gone by. Not that I am defender
Of total truth . . . like some . . . but I can say
With sweet immunity, in lines so true,
What gives me joy to utter, as to feel:
This love, mysterious, I have for you—
Far more than cognizance of your appeal:
The knowledge of the heart, as from a prior
Life—when? where?—(wonders your versifier).

In Celebration of the Day

We cannot fashion time, where in a whit
Doors close and open; nor can we know how
Once long ago (nine decades and a bit)
And many labyrinthine miles from now,
You fell into this world. And I, soon after,
Started my own complexity of travel
Through all the halls of learning: pain and laughter
Finding rooms of weaving and of ravel.

Of course I dare not say, as lovers do,
That it was fated that we find our way
To one another; but this I do find true—
I would no other, dear my friend, today:
You listen and reply, with care advising,
And call to tell me that the moon is rising.

On Staying Home from the Fair

Shall I compare thee to a summer's goat?
Not having gone to Fair called Common Ground,
I have no right to ape what William wrote
And say thou art more temperate and abound
In any kind of somewhat finer features—
So some might claim, but wrongly. Still I see
(However far removed from goat-shed bleachers)
My charming childhood pet's nobility.
'Tis true the horns of power do not grace
Thy handsome head, nor can thee walk on toe,
Nor sweetly bleat, and I could never place
A bell around thy neck: but this I know:
In summer, winter, autumn or the spring,
Change thee I would not, dear—for anything.

Doubly Glad

I went to find you—but you were not there.
Five minutes gone, I'd caught you from the car
In unexpecting glance: the golden air
Holding you in its arms: Ah, there you are!—
I felt, rather than thought. And then I thought
To walk, of sun-warmed banter, given, sought:
The laughter of two lifetime's winnowings.)

But you were gone. Still did the mindless light
Hum and linger where you had been sitting
For favored view (which lay, serene and bright,
Diminished not a white, so all unwitting).
When next we meet, I shall be doubly glad—
For presence, and for what we nearly had.

Comes Time

When it comes time to put his boat away
He buts a rowlock on his windowsill
Not so much, he tells me, against the chill
Before us, as a promise that a day
Will come. Considering the brave display,
I am encouraged to improve my skill
And weave my heart with threads of light, until
It sits in sun, and sings a roundelay.

Ask, how one manages through lonely snow?
With talisman—with promise—no regret
Coloring lovely air, for what was had.
So, quietly, we watch the long months go,
He has his rowlock—I, my amulet—
That we might winter over, and be glad.

Dear Friend

Dear friend, that when I question you reply
And that your answer comes before I send
And that we keep our converse, and know why,
Sets out an orchard I delight to tend,
For in the reaches of this husbandry
There hangs such fruit so heavy on the bough
That I, awakened, touch and taste and see,
Remember . . . what I never knew till now.

When others beckoned and I walked with them
Anonymous below the ghosting leaves
I could not find the apple on the stem,
Wandering in the half-light that deceives:
But with your coming, I to harvest came:
You are the only one to know my name.

The Cat's Dinner

Blue Bowls

My four cats
Well fed and clothed
Search for special pleasures:
Creamy film in my blue bowl,
Egg left on the fork.

This morning
I catch myself
Careful at every sip,
Turning and turning the cup
To name the flowers:

This old, fifth cat
Coming alert
To whatever small chance
Blooms half-hidden in sadness—
Finding a blue bowl.

The Familiar

Curving the cat
In heap of happy
As, days gone by,
Curled baby in belly—

Lacking new love
(Human for human)
You'll say—but I
(Wistful old woman)—

Grateful and glad
For fortune of fur
Changing a sigh
To pureness of purr.

My Pure Black Fur

Mouse-quick buried in her little paper
Handkerchief, curled in white box (some Christmas
Long ago, and oh, so soon forgotten) . . .

How easily the trowel slips the earth
Spring-viable, having awaited her
Through hungry winter heavy with frost . . .

How aptly sung her brief, light requiem
From a low branch now beginning its leaving
(Oh, splendid scarlet bird of unconcern) . . .

And how this shine of my pure black fur
Where I lie indolent in the window of blessings
Outshone her dull gray-brown
(Yet, sweetest glint of whiskers!)

When—last night—in shadow I found her—
When that cowering breast
And eyes' final fear aroused my flesh:
(How her availance drove me mad with love!)

Latest Advisements

Luka-in-the-Morning rises
From his corner of my bed,
Ready for the great surprises
That he hopes are just ahead:

Stretches, yawns and strolls demurely
To his kibbled bowl, where he
Takes one sniff. Then, he is purely
Filled with howl, advising me

That remains of last night's supper—
Nothing better, nothing more—
Leave him in a proper scupper,
Finding life a total bore.

Now I must, without impinging
On his rights of domicile,
Mention that his constant binging
Drags us to the needy file,

And point out that a foreclosure—
Lack of roof, no winter heat—
Would prove worse for his composure
Than a lack of breakfast treat.

Morning Story

California Cat, now stars have fled,
Exits his haven on the guest room bed
And sashays down, with self-important stroll,
To slake his thirst at the communal bowl
But finds, to his chagrin, the feline font
Being addressed by his sister from Vermont.

Approaching from behind, he patiently
Sits a brief moment, then (such fun to see!)
Decides enough's enough: stands tall and moves
To close encounter, that distinctly proves
Time's up.

Not so! He sniffs her little rump,
But, getting nowhere fast, proceeds to bump.
She hesitates just long enough to elicit
His frightful "MI-AOW!" (no one alive could miss it),
Meaning, we must assume, "Get the hell out
Of my imperial way!"
There is no rout.

Miss Green-State stretches . . . sidles out the door,
Mewing, "Good day." The California boor,
Barely glancing (having attained his wish)
Toward water bowl—heads for the kibble-dish.

Sextets & Such

When people struggle to define what "sex" is,
The varied use of such a world perplexes:
Sexton, Sexagenarian, sex-foil, sextuplets—
Complex enough to compose heroic couplets!—
It's in Middlesex (sounding a bit ambivalent).
As for the sense that grants great titillation,
I'll here relate a well-known observation:
The more a girl's exposed to "red-hot lovers,"
The faster and more surely she discovers
Behavior they proclaim to be "expert" in
More than not, is one they are inert in!
And men—the shy one whom you find alluring
May yet portend a partnership enduring—
For my sweet mother taught me long ago
To be, in public, English as the snow;
While in the privacy of one's boudoir
One may do as the French—and go as far.
So among you all, I court a nonchalance;
But with my spouse? Ah—vive la différence!

Lines Found

My name is Rosamond. I spell these lines
In hope that one—someone—will find their place
(How many years?)—lost, hidden in old vines

Enveloping my story, without trace—
And count the final cost of what I owe . . .
(Are you the one? Led, finally by grace?)

Widow of long-licentious lord, I go
With broken walk to sit beside his grave,
Deep in my weeds (at last!)—a proper show.

I gave him many sons; but one I gave
To him who could not take—yet had me all
Already, in a love we could not stave.

Promised at birth, I would not let them call
My heart to heel, nor keep me from a joy
Which neither prayers nor warnings could forestall . . .

When I was brought to bed of that fair boy
One name I uttered—once—in dire distress—
My single sound was key to Satan's ploy:

Dead, my two loves—and my lord turned merciless:
Oh, God!—would I had shared his sword's caress!

Ships That Pass . . . (at Eighty-Three)

You tell me that we met once, long ago—
A dance in Cleveland. Well, I never went
To Cleveland, nor attended, that I know,
A single dance (being incompetent).
But I know you. One glance through your disguise
Told me our spirits for ten thousand years
Have danced together as a compromise
To guard our passion as it disappears
Into the dark—again.

Come now, admit
My crooked smile, my creaky laugh, are nice
Enough to keep you warm, at least a bit.
And as for me, I'd have you in trice.

Sweet man, let's make our vessels run aground,
That we may waltz to bed, this time around.

A Dental Ode (for Bruce Verrill)

I love my Bruce, I love my Verrill!
For him I'd leap to give referral!

The tooth that breaks, the tenuous filling
Need his attentions (always willing).

True: prognoses, often chilling,
Sometimes lead to fearful billing . . .

But—!

Many fine fellows have come my way,
Yet, NONE, before, has thought to say

Those words most sweet, those words most thrilling:

"That's all the drilling!"

Confession of an Old, Female Half-Hippie

I did NOT burn my bra when we were doing it.
Pray, don't enquire my reasons for eschewing it:
Husband's disapproval, doubles, looming
(Affection for that man all else subsuming).

It's difficult to be a proper rebel:
Entanglement in love's seductive web will
(Especially if mutual) obscure
Nearly all need to render the world secure
From various ills . . . Alas, despite desire
This half-rebel never became entire,
Through simple laziness.
Yet now, at last,
I have achieved that symbol from the past:
Manumission: but never struck a match!

In truth, the teensy hooks are hard to latch
With these old hands and eyes—and in an hour
Charms of lift and support begin to sour.

Thus, in my effort to come clean, en route
To paradise, confession I salute:

Bra-less I stand, but not in freedom's fashion:
Only, that now, comfort's my ruling passion.

Crone's Wines

Search

I looked for the moon
But she was not there:
I thought: Too soon!
I thought: Elsewhere!

I knocked at the gate
Where the wise men are:
They said: Too late!
They said: Too far!

Then an old Crone said:
Give over the skies—
Go look instead
Where your heart lies.

So I looked within
And the moon comes bright—
Here rise my kin
And my delight.

Crone's Wines

Drink light of sun,
Barely edging the curve of the cat's shoulder!
There. You have won
Another minute's race (though both are older).

Drink, also, beam
Of sun, revealing blood within your fingers.
Deathless they seem!
(And are, these moments while the found hand lingers).

Drink deep, drink slow,
My little—and recall how carelessly
You ran to go
Into a future which would never be.

Remember that
Your small, brief worlds will alter, when you will die
(Or, when the cat).
Drink, carefully, these wines which clarify.

An Octogenarian Homily

Three states there be:
The good, the bad, and—in between
What the old wise ones, with their key,
Labeled the Golden Mean.

If we are smart
We will, at last when we are old,
Look sharp, wise up, and take to heart
The value of that special Gold.

From a Heavy Winter

Come, spring, and soon—yet—not too soon.
Come slow—with winter lingering
As you begin our longed-for boon
Teasing—a light snow fingering.

Do not rush into flowers that smother
Hesitant buds—oh, unsurpassed!—
That I, who may not see another,
May look lingering—look her last.

All Hallows

Leaves call me out.
They are the calling
As they are leaving:

Find what we are about!
See us, save us, falling!
Comfort our fear, our grieving!

Do not think it is wind.
Science is wrong in this.
Desire drives them on,

Longing, their reckless spin
Seeking a touch, a kiss
Before the clutch of gone.

I could go out and stride
Their fearful ways, to share
Their glorious end in gold—

But I am safe inside.
I have gray grief to bear
And my own death to hold.

In My Mirror

This is the face that launched five lovely ships.
Not one returned—each one, a perfect bird,
Coped with the crossing. How my old brain dips
And swirls, these days!—whatever I've averred
Could be all wrong!—likewise, the things we know
And I disclaim, could very well be true,
Leaving me in a pickle—this is so,
But—I don't care! Let me explain to you:
This little mirror came to me when we
Were far too young to journey to the feast;
Always she did her very best to be
As charming as the nature of the beast
Could easily allow—now, my great age
Laughs at the gray glass, and the wrinkled page.

Consideration of Weather

Waking to mist and fog,
My breath, my thought, hard-got:
Are we, indeed, that frog
Crouched in the gradual pot?

Why do our winds not blow,
Nor clouds let down their rain
Nor dwindle, that the glow
Of heaven may grow our grain?

Perhaps it has begun!
Perhaps some beggared soul
Thinking to best the sun
Will reach a terrible goal.

Soon we will hear the word
Come trumpeting, the name
By all, in trembling, heard:
Sweet, ultimate form of fame

None other can acquire
As fatal spark is hurled:
The pinnacle of fire—
To cinder away the world.

Death Watch

The way certain small clouds
Sail across stars

Even the smell of very old pines
After rain

And the way they move
Slow in the wind
The way they move
In the wind's love

They help me, yes they do.

They will have to help me
Bringing the wind and the stars

Into my hands.

Staircase

What does it say to me?
Light that comes through
The west window
At four, at five
Of the good clock,
Stroking the white spokes
(They go up and down)

Dark steps going up,
White spokes coming down?

Are they too quiet?

Do they say softly it will be enough—
All of this
Moving into me
It will have to be enough—

I tell them, say
Out loud
So they can hear

I'm listening, I'm listening,
I'm here and listening,
Just tell me, tell me,

Dark steps going down.

Dark's Wall

Beyond this window comes the night,
All around this house will stand
Darkness sheltering from light
Those who move on hidden land,

Yet I have no cause to walk
Safe from other eyes in shade:
In this laughter and this talk
In my sanctuary made:

For beyond this lighted room
There is nothing but a wall
Deep in terror, wide in doom
And topless tall.

You Know Who You Are

Friends: women, men: living and dying and dead,
Taken so variously to this single
Heart through grateful years, that we might mingle
As best we may; some of my sometimes bed
Or simply longed for: some who soul to soul
Mated and fled; or wandering, forget;
Or we, alas, let slip the magic knot:
I raise my glass!

And there's an honor roll
For those who (past and present and to come—
My hardy loves) for decades long have clung
Despite my sins, to joys we had when young
(Or younger). But for all, not just for some:
Should any friend precede me—wella, welladay!
This be my touch, my kiss . . . though far away.

Song at the Shore

Oh, does this beach remember
Her steps upon the sand
In April—in November
Her walks along the strand?

And does the beach grass tremble
To write her name again
In letters that resemble
The circles of amen?

Are not the rock-pools waiting
To catch her questing face?
Perhaps the sea, narrating
Her story in this place?

For she whose life was only
A white shell tossed by waves
Has gone, dispersed and lonely,
And lies in ocean caves.

Leo under the Snow

Let the Earth take now
What belongs to Earth:
Only She knew how
To bring you to birth.

Only She took care
To design your eyes
So the ancient stare
Of wisdom could rise,

And color your heart
Where waiting it lay—
And this is the part
That will always stay:

I will keep it clear,
The gift that you gave:
In my arms, ever near,
Kind, forgiving and brave.

While my days go on
And memory stands,
You will not be gone—
Safe under my hands.

Whatever Weather

In early youth, she'd say, to quell our doubt,
An authoritative person in a book
Bid her, whatever weather, to go out
On every day, to listen and to look—
Taste, if possible—and certainly, smell
And definitely feel beneath her feet
The real world. From cottage, from hotel,
She never failed: sand, soil or concrete.
In later years, on deep, enquiring trips
To trace old, honored sites of ancient pillage,
She loved even the turns on decks of ships,
The quiet stroll through the remotest village.
Though found, at end, lifeless upon her floor,
I know she'd walked up to the Golden Door.

Toward Helicon

Weathered and wise,
The great ones fall—
But in their rise
We triumph, all,
Able to keep
Their thought, their talk.

Though still we sleep,
In dreams we walk
Up hills of light
Toward Helicon!

Though it be night
They lead us on
Still beckoning
Through the dark wood—
Past reckoning:
The brave, the good.

Regarding Mary

Vivid as poppies in a farmer's field,
Forthcoming as the simple call of crows,
She was like sunlight breaking through the clouds
To spark the autumn leaves in Mary's Wood,

And toward wherever she is now—or, not,
As she said would be (rational, downright)—
We send our love, and harbor memories
Of this rare woman, wonderful as stars.

Dreaming the Dead

I stood at window, watching, waiting, swept
By autumn's grief, by longing so profound
That now, quiescent, I no longer wept.

Beyond the wide flat lawn of dying ground
There was a wood, and suddenly I knew
Unseen arrival, hidden, without sound.

Distant despair: I could not reach for you,
Tried to call out, knowing I could not call.
At last, a kind of understanding grew:

You had not come to me—there was a will:
But ways . . . You gathered sticks to build a fire
Beside a pool under a waterfall.

I knew your careful flame would climb no higher
Below the glory of October trees
Than what the warmth for chilled skin would require

After your dive and bathe . . . I saw, with ease,
The lesson brought: in water we are kin.

Your fire put out, acceptance stayed within.
And you were gone, so eager to begin.

Elegy in November

Now you are gone, dear one. Did you forget
To place your rowlock on the windowsill—
As you explained to me when first we met,
"A token of summer days at last"—oh, Bill,
How could I not love you as I took
That courage into me, those lonely days,
And learned my courage? For the little book
Lying upon your table spoke your ways,
Showed me your mind and heart. I will not cease
To call, "The moon, the moon!" when she shall rise
Over the river, full, and wrapped in peace:
Remembering how the spirit in your eyes
Approached the truth, by love of beauty driven,
And wisdom—carefully gathered—quietly given.

My Wall

I called him to me. I was very clear.
Build me a wall, I said. He smiled to hear.
A fine young man. He made me want to ask,
Why aren't you over there, doing your task?
Why aren't you over there—killing a few
Human beings, before they kill you?
That is necessity: kill your own brother,
Sister, daughter, son—your father, mother.

Of course, I didn't. It is not the kind
Of thing one says (whatever comes to mind).

Build me a wall, I said. A wall of stone.
He readily agreed. No undertone
To startle him—so far. But then I said:
We need it to memorialize the dead:
Each stone a body; for each skull a rock
(The babies', smaller, yes). A stumbling block
May be adherence to the building code
I want it down the middle of the road—
Route One, perhaps—that motorists might know
Death's visage, as they travel to and fro . . .

He'd quietly withdrawn, of course, by now.
I heard his truck start up. I woke, somehow.

I guess he thought that I had just gone mad,
Stark, staring crazy. As, indeed, I had.

Hands Beneath Head

Lying like this, I think I am
A girl again: that lightness, lightness.
Or, rather, feel—
It is the body only that knows this:
Smoothed-out skin of belly; opening lungs
Looking at all, like flowers;
Most of all the stretch along the breasts
Unused again. Lover and child-quiet.

Lying like this I'm minded of the monks
Approaching death, asking to be moved
(So I've been told)
From bed to floor.
Perhaps I'll want that, too.
One could not ask for more.
Wouldn't that be a readying?
All gone, all new:

Setting sail
Into the winds of possibility.

A Painting with Final Colors

Smoothed, her blue pillow (wrought with willow's
Gray-green leaves), lying by one who grieves
Beside the yellow daisies' glow
While another—sister? mother?
Daughter?—pours the silver water
From the old jug, violet, gold:
Murmured partings' murmurings.

Persian lilies, in this version
Echoing clovered coverlet,
Hum as orange, grape and plum
Lend gentle voices to the blend
That, symphony for all to see,
Carries the grace of final colors
Soft as soft breath, to her new death.

Leo at Leaf-Fall

Hail and farewell
Within the wood—
If all goes well,
As well it should:

Farewell and hail
Across the field—
What year would fail
Another's yield?

In world without,
In world within:
Some roundabout
Continues spin.

Some lofty round
So keeps us humble:
Ah, here—we bound,
Ah, here—we stumble.

And, though we weep,
Bidding adieu,
We break new sleep
To wake anew

And know again
(Not overmuch)
He joys of then:
The look, the touch,

The shapes of love:
This great . . . that small:
The fitting glove,
The answering call.

Little Elegy/Little Jubilee

This golden candle, living, moving, dancing
As you no longer are—
Having embarked (oh, earliest! only glancing!)
Upon a wandering star—

May this small flame guide spirit into clay:
Come find you in the vast
And wrap you in our love, and lead the way
And bring you home—at last.

Dear Aria! You found the candle's flame
I sent to find you (far
Within the dark, alone, without a name,
Riding your tiny star)—

Ah, you remembered how we longed to hold
Happiness unbeknown—
You followed flame to find the love foretold,
Your heart within our own.

The Twins

This is the day
(Or else tomorrow)
When we will pay—
No joy: no sorrow.

Gone is the night:
Here morning rises
Bringing to light
Her own devices.

This afternoon
Come bees to clover
In honeymoon
(Or—is it over?)

Our conjoined twins:
No sorrow: no joy:
The skull that grins
At the archer boy.

Circle-Dance

My rooms, by water, show
That I from water came
As did we all the same
And all to water go:

My windows saying (never
Far from their refrain
Of river, mist, or rain):
All bodies—howsoever

Lying in earth or tide—
Must rise again, somewhere:
We willy-nilly share
The waltz of planet's ride.

All spirits, too, released
From troublings of their stay
Will find, in tango's way,
New famine—and new feast:

Dancing into the round,
Triumphant in the mesh
That holds new water's flesh
Risen again from ground.

Three Mothers

I lay inside my darling mother
Warm embraced the sun of her womb,
Content to hear the seed of her singing
And thread my loom.

I lie inside my darling Mother
Here where Her shuttle voices move,
Content to sing the web of our weaving
And learn Her love.

I'll lie inside my darling Mother
Deep and deep when the leaves fall—
Content to sleep in that silent music
And wait Her call.

Supplicant

Mother of All, Mother of Light
Maker of mysterious fire,
In your persuasion's gentle might
Lead us from habit and desire:
Draw us awake who hourly sleep
Forgetful of a fall from grace:
Burn through covering clouds that keep
Us from the vision of your face.

Bring back the balance of belief
That All is One (the live, the dead),
That those whom we have brought to grief
Or will indeed—being comforted
Under your hand—forgive and heal—
Forgiven—all, around the wheel.

Just before Midnight

Say Goodnight! to this good night—
She'll cradle us, cradle us
In the arms of cool delight
As the years enable us
So to leave, and love again:

We who do not ask for more:
And the Goddess be as kind
As she has been heretofore
That we love and be not blind,
That we leave and love again—

Merry meet, and love again.

When Will She Turn

Old woman tumbled in her dreams
Ready at midnight, under the far
Cold stars above the river—are
Still some losses tangled in the beams
Of her waning moon?—

(Or even in the sun
Soon to begin to rise higher than moon
Over the warming fields where soon
Even the losses will have won.)

When will she turn again to earth?
What new beginning—in what womb
Engendered in her own sweet tomb?

Old woman tumbling into birth . . .

At Sunrise

Turning now, as I sleep, I take
Across my eyes the silent word
Given by old Sun's golden bird.

Learning, I have longed to shake
An apple from the sacred tree
That turns sleep into unity
Before the true daybreak:

Yearning, at end, at least to make
My entrance in a gown of light
Woven of day, woven of night—
Hearing, at last, "Awake!"

On That Last Stone

Called "beautiful," I only knew they lied,
Having looked in the mirror, as also
"Brave" could not be taken, since inside
Slow creatures crept through grasses, quick to know
My broken limbs. Within the glass I saw
Accidental shape of flesh on bone
(Lineaments the darkened centuries draw)
But found my guarded eyes—afraid, alone.

Few can define the place, the hour, when first
We offer ourselves to lions, and forgive
Necessities of hunger and of thirst
Like to our own, allowing all to live.
Therefore, on that last stone, they might engrave:
"She moved toward beauty, as she grew more brave."

Maggie Finch with a note she kept in her wallet
(Photo by Annie Finch)

Maggie Finch was born Margaret Rockwell on April 20, 1921. Her poems have appeared in publications such as *The Christian Science Monitor, Saturday Review,* and *Sequoia,* and her three previous books of poems are *Davy's Lake, The Barefoot Goose,* and *Sonnets from Seventy-Five Years.* She has served as president of the National Institute of American Doll Artists and copresident of the Maine Poets Society.